D1602979

the
UNTAMED
ELEMENTAL

Tasya van Ree

ROOST BOOKS

To my family, behold the jewel within. I will hold this gift in reverence and promise to always speak with the richness of a prolific hand.

Kiki, my soul, my bridge to the animal kingdom, thank you for your mastery and benevolent teachings.

To my divine feminine, the universe is your form. For all lifetimes, I love you.

To my divine masculine, we have been incarnated as artists. Two birds forever.

My highest gratitude to Safia, a bright star whose understanding of all worlds guided my heart's voice into a transcription of structural beauty.

Introduction

Incantations for Revelation

Your soul knows the way already. *The Untamed Elemental* simply offers it a spectrum of color and linguistic geometry that, combined with your intention, awakens your own inner guidance system to help navigate all of life's passages through the unknown. As a companion for your intuition and intellectual heart, this deck is composed of fifty-two cards, each representing a facet of Earth's medicine in a union of visual and written motifs of the natural world designed to unlock lost remembrances of cosmic truths. As your relationship with this deck grows, perpetual self-discovery unfolds and the voice of your inner mystic becomes stronger.

Before You Begin

These cards assign gender-specific personal pronouns to earthly elements. With the understanding that nature is not conditioned by concepts of gender, this deck acknowledges that all of life contains creative energies we refer to as masculine and feminine in order to categorize and understand them. The use of *he* and *she* in the descriptions of the cards is a nod to the creative polarity required for life to exist and is given intuitively to each subject based on the essence of the qualities it represents. This is not meant to constrain any part of nature with a binary gender assignation. You are invited to interpret the cards in a way that is meaningful and authentic to your own intuitive understanding.

The Elements

This deck is organized by the five elements—Earth, Water, Air, Fire, Ether—as they are represented in the systems of Ayurveda. While these cards exist outside these systems of ancient wisdom, each modality uses the elements as a useful reference point to holistically connect with our planet and our bodies. This structure can help you identify themes and patterns in your own readings based on the energetic principles of nature. It also offers guidance for understanding any asymmetry and balance in your circumstances. For example, drawing cards that are mostly from one element might offer important information about what you may require to harmonize your situation.

EARTH

Grounding and forgiving, Earth is the element of innocence, safety, and foundational support. Earth is the
primary starting point for life in physical form. It gives
us the terra firma on which we can evolve and grow;
its kindheartedness is that of a loving mother. With too
much Earth we may feel trapped and claustrophobic.
This can be offset by connecting with universal wisdom. Not enough Earth may allow the vibration of fear
to dominate our experience. Find balance by connecting with the Earth. This is easy to do by walking through
nature or moving the body in dance.

WATER

Water is the navel of pleasure and the wellspring of
emotions. Rivers and seas form a relational network,
transporting intelligence for the sole purpose of creation. Water's balanced nature is flow and ease. It offers
an accurate reflection of our inner landscape: too
much and we become overwhelmed, drowning in our
feelings and unable to progress, but too little causes
our creativity to wither. Balance the Water element on
both sides of the equation by channeling emotions into
creativity of any constructive kind.

AIR

Incalculable and soaring, Air is the element of the visionary. The Air element is necessary for new creation, wider possibilities, and expanded thought. Too much Air will result in flightiness and the inability to birth vision into existence. Balance an excess of Air element by connecting your body with the Earth through walking barefoot or simply lying on the ground. Not enough Air element creates stagnation and myopia. To balance a deficit of Air, tune in to your breath long enough that it becomes meditative and you feel the expansiveness and levity of being well oxygenated.

FIRE

Expressing magnitudes of heat, Fire is the planetary metabolic principle. Fire's flames digest, transform, destroy, and bestow life; they radiate our determination and self-esteem. We invoke Fire's passion when we require the personal power to create. We solicit Fire's absolution when we are called to purify stories that no longer serve us. When there is too much Fire, we find ourselves embroiled in existential argument, but when there is not enough Fire, we lack the will to persevere. To amplify the Fire element, spend time in the sun; to quell it, immerse the body in cooling Water.

ETHER

As the elemental firstborn, Ether is the holder of consciousness. Neutral and omniscient, Ether is both the scribe and library for all of existence. Ether is the space that all the other elements fill—it is the pause between notes of music and the moment before an inhale becomes an exhale. Etheric imbalances can feel either like a lack of purpose or being too busy—both of which are symptoms of overstimulation. The Ether element can be brought into attunement with sounding, humming, or singing.

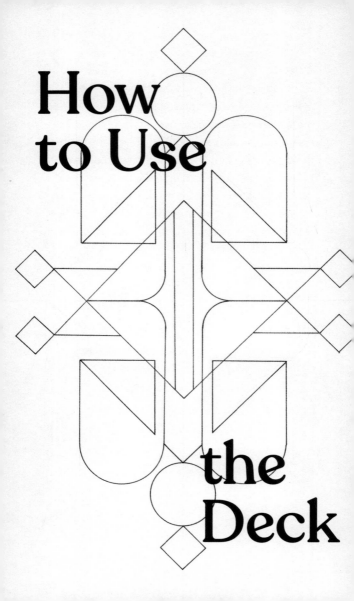

How
to Use
the
Deck

THESE CARDS offer a ritual for working with the healing frequencies of the elements to develop a deeper relationship with your spirit. To collaborate most effectively with the deck, you will want to bring your full attention to it, as you might in meditation. Take a few moments to sit in silence before you begin. Your undiluted awareness is the investment you make to receive its accurate counsel.

Bring breath and curiosity to your sessions with the deck, and it will reveal its trustworthy guidance. Each time you work with it, focus on your intention and desired trajectory. Form a question that is specific to your circumstances and open to the unexpected, mystical observations you most require. Serendipity and opportunity are everywhere. When we allow ourselves to be surprised by wisdom, we align with its magic. Before reading about the cards' meaning, sit with the ones you have drawn and allow unconditioned insights to come to you. After your personal contemplation, use this companion book to enrich your interpretations.

A note about shuffling and cutting the deck: Eventually you will discover your preferred method of shuffling. If you are a beginner, keep it simple, and use an overhand shuffling technique by cutting the deck approximately in half and placing one section on top of the second and then repeating. Be sure to mix the cards well, especially before your first use. It is important to shuffle the deck before each reading while repeating your question in your mind. This will help you select the most relevant cards for your circumstances.

A note on balance: Sometimes you will draw an upside-down card. This is not considered an error. Rather, an upside-down card indicates there is an imbalance or block in the area of your life it represents. Drawing an upside-down card is an opportunity to look at any unconscious commitments you have to staying stuck or disempowered. For example, drawing an upside-down Butterfly, which represents meta-morphosis, could indicate that there is part of you that is resisting evolution or change. Perhaps you are sabotaging your evolution by refusing to slow down and go into your cocoon so that transformation can take place. Suggestions for rebalancing are included in the cards' descriptions.

Daily Card Meditation

Simple and elegant, a daily card meditation offers prescient guidance for the daily events you may encounter and how to orient yourself to the tasks at hand. As part of your morning meditation, shuffle the deck and then select a card. Gaze at it for a few moments, then close your eyes and imagine stepping into the card, as if you were entering a new dimension. Ask the element or animal represented in the card what information or gift it has for you. Then give yourself enough time in your meditation for it to answer.

Past/Present/Future Meditation

Shamanic and efficient, this three-card spread allows you to see the past dynamic, present circumstance, and future outlook of a situation. Opening a space for understanding the past allows you to shift future probabilities by acting in the current moment. In this way, you are aligning with forces more powerful than space and time to help shape your world. Activate your intention for this three-card draw either by shuffling the deck once in the beginning or between each card you select. Then choose three cards, one at a time, and place them facedown in a row from left to right. As you draw the first card, focus on receiving information about the essence of the past with regard to your situation. Intend that the next card you select will clarify the present quality of your subject. Ask for the future outlook to be revealed in your third card. Once you have your three cards, turn them over in order of past, present, and future and viscerally receive the insights that arise from both their content and how they relate to each other.

Merkaba Sleep Meditation

Your Merkaba body is your light or spirit body. While your physical body sleeps, your light body can activate profound healing if you program it to do so. Before bed, shuffle the deck and then draw a card for guidance about a situation in your world that requires mending. Place the card under your pillow or on your nightstand and intend that your Merkaba body will work with the energy of the card while you sleep.

The Five-Card Divination Meditation

This draw is perfect for an anniversary or birthday to divine the theme of your own forthcoming year, or turn to it on New Year's Day to activate possibilities for and receive information about the seasons that are about to unfold. Activate this five-card draw either by shuffling the deck once in the beginning or between each card you select. Choose four cards, one representing each three-month cycle in the upcoming year. The fifth card is for the overall theme of your year, and it should be positioned above your four-card arrangement. Notice any themes that arise, seeing if the elements are equally represented or if one in particular is more abundant. This will give you information about bringing in balance. For example, drawing three Fire cards could indicate that you might benefit by introducing more cooling Water meditations or activities to your overall year.

The Tonic Meditation

This two-card draw offers a remedy if you are experiencing some kind of spiritual, mental, or physical obstacle. Shuffle the deck and, as you draw two cards, ask the first card to show you the essence of the path. This card indicates its highest purpose in your life if the path ahead of you unfolds without obstacle. It points to your soul's true desire for experiencing the situation and offers meaning that transcends the preferences of the ego, aligning instead with your greater evolutionary path. If, for example, you want to receive information about closing a business deal and you draw Crystal, it could indicate that the transaction is linked with your soul's desire to heal an aspect of your inner life, such as

self-confidence. Ask the second card, placed perpen-
dicularly across the top of the first card, to reveal the
obstacle or imbalance. This card points to not only the
block but also how you can release or balance it. For
example, if you use the Tonic Meditation to receive
information about calling in a new love and you draw
Ray of Light as the second card, it could indicate it's
time to place your attention on what you most desire,
rather than what you aren't currently experiencing. Or
if you are looking to receive clarity about whether or
not to take a job and you select the Moon card as your
second card, you might feel compelled to investigate
whether or not the job aligns with your values.

Earth

CRYSTAL

Crystal

SELF-HEALING   Crystal is an instrument of transcendence, an iconic talisman of the journey inward. Forged deep in the belly of Earth, she emerges clear and brilliant, emanating form and balance through her highly ordered expressions of the infinite. Her sacred geometries hold the planetary codes and cosmic blueprints of universal existence. She responds to your intentions to conserve, direct, transmit, and transmute energy. She is a powerful healing ally.

Crystal sends the message that self-healing is under way. You can amplify this progress by visualizing your wholeness and aligning with the curative frequencies freely given by Earth. Self-healing is a powerful choice. When its visualization is married with intuitive listening and a commitment to self-kindness, improvement becomes inevitable. If you choose to work with a physical crystal, trust her purity and light to guide you home to yourself.

Balanced: faith in Earth's energies and your ability to heal yourself

Imbalanced: fear of the body, fear of the Earth

To bring into balance: work with crystals, walk steadily on the Earth

ELEPHANT

Elephant

COMPLEXITY Elephant is a steadfast monarch, matriarch, and servant. Royal by nature, her presence is felt as the trumpets announce her determined march. She is loyal and devoted to elders and children alike and reminds us that the way we choose to exercise our power influences how those around us will wield theirs. A true leader, she leaves a deep footprint for others to follow so they don't lose their way.

Majestic Elephant is a reminder that more than one thing can be true. She asks you to validate your wild, dynamic, creative desires while also honoring your fears. She wants you to set aside linear thinking and welcome support from your ancestors. She courts you to honor two seemingly opposing truths with the same degree of respect. Free yourself from seeing the world through a binary lens and allow the fullness of your complexity to pour forth. This radical act of self-acceptance removes the obstacles that might have once seemed insurmountable. It opens the door to miracles. Most importantly it paves the way to your wholeness.

Balanced: curious, accepting, regal, sovereign

Imbalanced: radicalized perspectives, stuck in circular thinking

To bring into balance: gift-giving, acts of service, acceptance of self and others even if it feels unwarranted

GAZELLE

Gazelle

CHANGE OF DIRECTION Gazelle dances across the continental horizon, alert, light of foot, and vibrating with unopposed grace. His beauty is a spell cast upon the world. He approaches his environs with vigilance and is protected by the safety of the herd. As one, they strive with confidence and bravery, surviving via telepathic, innate communication. Gazelle's capacity for imaginative improvisation allows him to outsmart and outrun his predators. His name comes from the Arabic word *gazal*, meaning "love poem," and this light and fast animal is drawn to you when it's time to change direction.

When manifesting a desired outcome, there are phases when progress is slow or altogether absent. Gazelle suggests that sometimes a solution comes through a sudden shift in perspective. A fresh—and even drastically changed—outlook offers great inspiration. Move decisively in a new direction, and you have the opportunity to fall back in love with your original vision. Gazelle is a love poem—spontaneous and full of heart—and as you begin to embody these qualities, there is room for unimagined possibilities to emerge.

Balanced: flexible in your process, agile

Imbalanced: stagnant, lethargic, listless, indecisive

To bring into balance: write a love poem to your vision

Lynx

SACRED SILENCE Lynx stalks silently under the stars of the cold, northern midnight—a huntress at heart. Her thick fur, wide paws, and agile limbs allow her to traverse green forests, scale granite faces of mountains, and negotiate the freshly fallen snow. Echoes of the world are held at bay, for she has chosen solitude. She is completely at one with her habitat. Her independence comes without complication, and her silence remains solely her own.

Lynx calls upon you to hold sacred silence—at least for the time being. There is great power in keeping your own counsel when appropriate. Silence is particularly wise when applied to a new project, relationship, or vision that still lives in the gestational or liminal realms. This is because sacred silence is a womb where dreams and desires may come into material form. Go with Lynx into meditation, where the light of possibility will allow your dreams to unfurl. Trust that you will know when the time is right to speak. Have faith you'll understand exactly whom to share it with.

Balanced: discerning, intuitive, independent

Imbalanced: aloof, disingenuous, contemptuous

To bring into balance: keep your own counsel until you know the time is right to share

MOUNTAIN

Mountain

ALIGNMENT A vertical masterpiece of the natural world, Mountain obtains cosmic access and conducts the steadfast life force rooted in the center of Earth. He entices us with his ridges and vistas and demands coherence between conviction and action. He is proud of his statuesque prominence, embodying incorruptible dignity. Wisdom cultures have long been attracted to the wild embrace of Mountain's range of summits and extreme climates in the exploration of spiritual elevation and states of absolute consciousness.

Mountain urges you to focus on your alignment, particularly as it relates to your spine. Just as Mountain establishes a coherence of flow between planetary and cosmic energy, your spine both avails you to Earth frequencies and ensures you have access to heightened wisdom. Maintaining healthy alignment in your vertebrae will keep your body vital, your intuition activated, and your dignity intact. Our souls are honed by our physical systems, and your spine is an instrument through which you can manifest greatness.

Balanced: immaculate alignment between conviction and action

Imbalanced: directionless, lacking clarity of purpose, chronic back pain

To bring into balance: activate your essential self by embodying Mountain's unwavering dignity and stillness

Peacock

TRANSMUTATION   Peacock lives in the woods where he consumes, among other things, poisonous plants. His ability to transmute vegetal toxins into extravagant, iridescent plumage makes him an alchemist of the highest order. Peacock has a reputation for vaingloriousness. He is boastful, exuberant in his beauty, and has the mastery required to back up his outrageous self-assurance.

Peacock invites you to take in information or circumstances both negative and positive and alchemize them into a harmonized energetic field that blesses your life. To do this is to master the art of transmutation, and it requires accepting your pain with as much love and gratitude as you do your happiness. When you do this, you begin to experience everything in life as happening *for* you rather than *to* you. Your travails become a gateway to greater freedom and beauty. With the application of loving awareness, everything is energy just waiting to be liberated into a more authentic expression of itself.

Balanced: assigning sacred purpose to the entirety of your life
Imbalanced: feeling immobilized by your perceptions of your circumstances

To bring into balance: dedicate time to serve others with full openness and acceptance, become available to the deeper awareness that is waiting to be revealed

ROOT

Root

STABILIZATION   Root is the starting point. He is the vast, unseen network of life that draws energy from the Earth and creates a stable platform for life to grow and thrive. He offers a constant source of sustenance, connection, and communication. Root delves and twists, sharing insight with his neighboring kin and creating a strong community. As the most ancient and reliable anchor of planetary support, he guides us to grow stronger and more stable.

Root asks you to establish firm foundations and develop a relationship with your own network of stabilization. He is the connecting force that carries all answers, so take stock: Are you receiving the right nourishment? Are your relationships loving and supportive? Are you drinking enough water, getting enough movement and sleep, breathing deeply? These pleasurable and achievable practices should be your starting point. An imbalance in one of them will translate to depletion in other areas of your life. Nurture your roots and watch your life blossom in miraculous ways.

Balanced: flourishing, productive, effective

Imbalanced: depleted, inefficient, stunted, scattered

To bring into balance: explore nature in new ways while listening to your subtle body, initiate self-inquiry in all that arises for you

ROSE

Rose

UNDEFENDED HEART   Her delicate scent is a microcosm; it contains notes of the celestial bodies that have lent her their wisdom so that she may align herself with universal love. Between her golden center and thorns is a story of both praise and protection; she is the pristine flower of angelic adoration and is also endowed with the ability to draw blood from a mindless approacher. She is Rose, a potent aide for harmonizing the heart.

Rose requires both shadow and light to do her work: her medicine is strongest beneath a full moon. She speaks of love; within her realm, nothing else exists. The Earth journey is filled with joys and sorrows, and Rose asks you to draw upon her magic to live with an undefended heart. Take care to keep your heart center washed clean so that it doesn't close down from the exhaustion of being overburdened. Rose radiates purity and connects your entirety to this present moment, to her beloved garden, where you will return to harmony and balance. Communing with Rose is a powerful way to help maintain the alacrity of your heart through the ups and downs of life.

Balanced: keen emotional intelligence, openhearted

Imbalanced: blocked feelings, heady, bitter

To bring into balance: shift into your higher mind, validate your authentic feelings

Tree of Life

SELF-CORRECT   Holding the essential balance between Earth and Sky, Tree of Life forms a singular, ever-growing veracity of interconnectedness. He is blessed by the multitude of nutrients drawn through his roots and provides a strong and generous shelter of truth and perspective for all who seek refuge with him. He breathes and stands tall, offering a canopy of consciousness so that his essentia will be reborn for all eternity.

Tree of Life offers the blessing of his supportive system so that any imbalance in your life may self-correct. The answers you seek are within you, because you are the channel through which higher intelligence experiences itself. You are an emanation of your spirit's signature passed through a template of sacred geometry, the result of which is a rare, atomic form. All that you desire to experience is available now. The liberation you strive for is already here. Spend time connecting with Tree of Life in your daily meditation, and every aspect of your world will begin to come into greater alignment with your own internal truths.

Balanced: feeling supported by and connected to all life

Imbalanced: the perception of having to do it alone

To bring into balance: rest in the awareness that you are perfectly supported to live your life

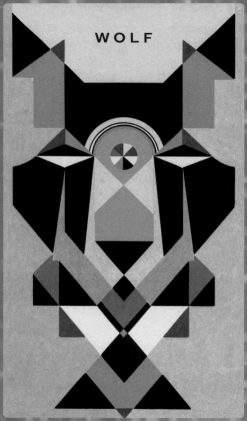

Wolf

AWAKEN YOUR WILDNESS   Wolf is a maternal ancestor from a loyal breed. Her unapologetic wildness is the result of always being tuned in to the subtle understanding of her instinctual impulse to survive. She is unimpeded by external forces. She trusts her own sharp temperament and mind and is inspired by the ritualistic aspect of the hunt.

Wolf guides you to awaken your wildness. It is time to unblock your whole inimitable and untamed self. Immerse your body in water; let it dry in the sunshine. Engage in conversation with loved ones, harmonize in song, stargaze, dance, welcome new ideas. What you lose in productivity you will make up for in the revival of dormant instincts that will guide you to make efficient, powerful choices. Nurture what your ancestral guides have instilled in you and trust the process. A journey into your free, authentic self awaits.

Balanced: keen, wise, purposeful

Imbalanced: blocked instinct, muted intuition

To bring into balance: become witness to the relationship between your conscious and subconscious mind; cultivate the relationship between your mind, body, and spirit

Water

MANTA RAY

Manta Ray

CALIBRATION   The grand Manta Ray soars through the water and even catapults himself into the air with fierce strength. His ability to gracefully maneuver comes from a deft internal temperature regulator and exceptional navigation skills. Moving with innate knowledge, Manta Ray is perfectly calibrated for his environment. Manta Ray sightings beckon you to break free from the obstacles that hold you back and reconfigure them for your greater good.

Manta Ray illustrates the importance of calibrating your life force so that you can experience more ease, grace, and freedom through the depths and surfaces of life. Shake off any negative energy that has accumulated on or around you. Make certain you are surrounded by positive, loving, encouraging relationships that reflect back your magnificence. Release anything that is draining your energy. Practice unconditional self-respect. These efforts will allow you to align with the natural flow and rhythm of life so that your time and energy are efficiently spent and you are more available for play and fun.

Balanced: playful, energized, in touch with your body's innate wisdom

Imbalanced: drained, overexertion, unnecessarily cautious

To bring into balance: find joy in simplicity and freedom in the complicated

OCTOPUS

Octopus

REGENERATION   As a complex master of disguise and charismatic contortionist, Octopus is ever-changing, highly resilient, and totally unlimited. She is an independent queen with three hearts, nine brains, and an incredible talent for regeneration. She is a vessel of everlasting treasures that fuel her total recovery and dispel perceptions of terminality.

As a living representation of the power of regeneration, Octopus bestows the auspicious news that, despite profound loss or wounds, life is dexterous. She supports the improbable truth that brokenness is not defeat; we can come back even stronger than before. Within the universe, there is an infinite supply of energy: money is not spent, it is circulated; love is never lost, it takes new forms; opportunities aren't missed, they return in ways that more accurately reflect your truth. Call on Octopus's medicine when you need to be reminded that healing and regeneration are not only possible, they are the nature of life itself.

Balanced: flexible, resilient, creative, regenerative

Imbalanced: struck down, contracted, brittle

To bring into balance: float or soak in water, anoint your body with precious oils

RIVER

River

FORGIVENESS   As in all life, River begins and ends at the source, polishing smooth all sharp opposition and offering generous opportunities to utilize her waters. She transforms and defines the landscape with her winding paths and gathering pools and acts as a meeting place for cleansing and quenching. Great civilizations have always been bound to her gifts; she is a timeless force. River is the living oracle of inter-connectedness; it is her healing waters that dispel our illusions of sin, our perceived separation from the divine. We look to her to mend our brokenness, just as blood mends a broken bone.

River appears when forgiveness is required. Whether someone deserves your forgiveness or not has no relevance; your decision to forgive is a gift you give to yourself. Release the poison of resentment and move in the direction of your choosing; no one outside of yourself has the power to allay your joy. Often, the most difficult person to forgive is oneself. This type of forgiveness requires special tenderness and care. Call upon River's unifying waters to wash away your misper-ceptions and forgive.

Balanced: self-responsibility, emotional and mental coherence
Imbalanced: blame and criticism toward self or others, harsh judgment

To bring into balance: become *willing* to forgive, even if it seems impossible

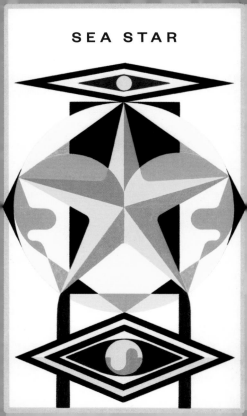

Sea Star

SIMPLICITY   As the night sky descends into water, his form is redefined through the lens of ancient eyes. Granular and spiny, Sea Star is a simple, elegant, and very necessary contributor to the abyssal depths he calls home. Constructed with overlapping armored plates, he moves through his world with impenetrable support. His slow-paced, oceanic rhythm matches his highly developed and profoundly sensitive nervous system. He is a keystone species, maintaining balance within his environment. In this way, Sea Star exemplifies a rarely observed truth: by simply being who you are, you are making a deeply valuable contribution.

Without hesitancy, Sea Star unseals the value of simplicity. He urges you to cease overthinking and, instead, trust. There are no improvements necessary before moving forward. Sea Star, who operates on the instinctual impulses he receives from his well-honed nervous system, doesn't analyze what he is going to do next; he simply does it. This natural responsiveness is what keeps him alive and well. Sea Star reminds you that your pure existence qualifies you as a valuable contributor to your community and the planet, and you don't have to attempt perfection in order to earn the right to be here.

Balanced: effortless effort, healthy instinct

Imbalanced: clutter, overthinking, overdoing

To bring into balance: trust your instinct

SEA URCHIN

Sea Urchin

PROTECTION   A spiky flower surrounds this alluring aquatic fossil. She is building her own energy supply, bearing witness to everything that surrounds her. Sea Urchin's fivefold symmetry makes her a study in the cosmic wonders of sacred geometry. As an ancient amulet of protection, she resurrects a sense of safety by dispelling negativity and clearing blockages to better strengthen a connection to source.

Sea Urchin is here to let you know that there are protective forces surrounding you, unseen but completely real. Your invisible security detail is always working to keep you safe. Your guardians are most effective at their jobs, however, when you establish clear lines of communication with them. You only need to ask for the guidance that will always ensure you are in the right place at the right time.

Balanced: confidence in your inherent safety

Imbalanced: fear as perpetual background noise

To bring into balance: regularly affirm that you live on a friendly planet and that it is safe to be in a body

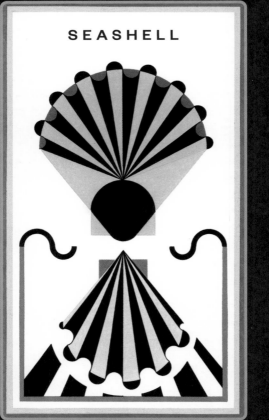

SEASHELL

Seashell

SPIRITUAL GROWTH   Her nautical structure is immaculate; she is an evolutionary protector of life. Seashell is born with precision, forged to embody robust stability. Carried by waves and tides, she is a guardian of life, promoting harmonious tranquility and the sincere, courageous benevolence of spiritual growth. She is definite and unparalleled.

Seashell is an auspicious insignia of your unfolding evolution and validates that you are on a path of true spiritual development. Spirit enlists Seashell's immaculate design and ability to weather myriad conditions as a metaphor, asking that you recognize all things as coming from the same source of intelligence that generates, organizes, and dissolves the entirety of life in this universe. If you choose it to be so, every loss, mistake, fear, pleasure, and reckoning are in service to your self-realization. At this point in your evolution, it is impossible for you to leave the path. With that in mind, why not enjoy the full, beautiful evolutionary experiment? Rest in the unshakable truth that you are traveling upward on a golden spiral and there's no going back.

Balanced: embracing unmitigated growth

Imbalanced: only accepting certain, preferred circumstances as being spiritual

To bring into balance: give yourself permission to enjoy and embrace all of life

Swan

SOUL MATE   Soft, white curves delineate his superior angle; there is no other like him. He is an artist and the epiphany of grace. Swan is devout in his perpetuity. He mates for life, choosing his companion with discernment. They are two lovers but one being, connected by a single stream for all eternity. Together, they create dynasties of beauty. His memory is long, and his love never ceases. Vast wings shelter his young and carry him with great speed across the sky.

Swan indicates the presence of a soul mate. To sound, sing, and be reflected by the sonnet and voice of another—this is a rarity. Whether this person has arrived into your life as a romantic partner or not, they have something to offer you on a quantum level. You made an agreement with them, long before you were born, to serve each other in this lifetime. Bless this one, for they are here to help you cultivate the elegance of your spirit.

Balanced: maintaining sovereignty in the intensity of a soul mate connection

Imbalanced: losing one's self in the ardent reflection of another

To bring into balance: stay present with yourself while in the company of others

WATERFALL

Waterfall

LET GO   Waterfall is an indigenous offering as resounding as the hum of the Earth. She calibrates and transforms all who witness her. An azure-colored force field—pulsating with purity, obeying the gravitational pull of her destiny, and shaping the Earth along the way—she dances with glittering abundance. Waterfall, in her unhinged impermanence, shows us that some things cannot be stopped. It is through her wild existence that we receive a transmission: what has passed will be reborn by plunging into the soothing depths of euphoria. All we have to do is let go.

Waterfall says that nothing is permanent, and so grasping is pointless. This is actually good news. It takes so much effort to hold on tightly, and doing so rarely yields the desired result. Imagine you are thirsty and have only your hands from which to drink. If they are fists, the water has no place to rest long enough to make it into your mouth. But if you open your hands gently, a natural reservoir forms, and you will be able to quench your thirst. Take a cue from Waterfall and release what you have in your fists. Just like her trajectory, that of your destiny is unstoppable. What is truly yours will come without constriction.

Balanced: frequent synchronicity and new opportunities
Imbalanced: grasping, controlling, repeating the same story
To bring into balance: let go where you are overly attached

Wave

UNITY   Wave's duration is unbounded; he loops consistently within his own tempo. He is fearless and valiant, peaking repeatedly through constant diligence. Forged by Wind and initiated by Moon, he is a conundrum, both distinct and inseparable from the ocean. Each Wave is unique and yet emanates from and returns to his mother element. His potential manifests as an eternal now.

Wave rolls in as a reminder that you are part of something much greater than your individual life. You are a fantastic and improbable expression of existence. The creative force that generates and organizes the life of every animal, star, snowflake, plant, and nebula in the universe also chose to experience itself, uniquely and beautifully, as you—and vice versa. Knowing yourself as an autonomous but inseparable participant in all of life helps allay painful perceptions of separation from others and even unclaimed parts of yourself. It opens you to the truth-filled salve that it is safe to rest into your innate and magnificent connection with your wholeness and all of life.

Balanced: an enjoyable sense of connection with one's self
Imbalanced: loneliness and isolation, a pervasive mistrust of one's intuition

To bring into balance: the sound of ocean waves balances the brain's hemispheres and helps bring forth an awareness of unity consciousness

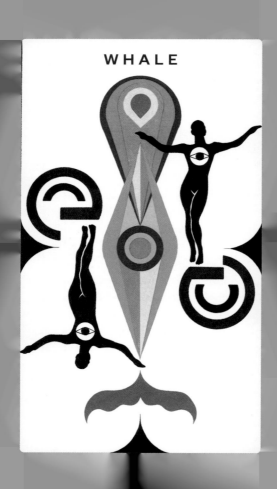

WHALE

Whale

COMMUNICATION   Vibrations of melodic patterns pulsate through his element, echoing and resounding in harmony. Whale swims to remote destinations, expressing a composed symphony that keeps Earth's magnetic fields in balance. He sends his calls far and wide by pressing his mouth to the ocean floor, summoning and selecting his mate through audible transference. He seduces with caution and tenderness; the magnetism of two hearts beating as one is real—a recognition exchanged. When there is an authentic connection, there is familiarity with one's self as much as with the other. His is the language of honesty, of transparency.

Whale calls you to dive deeper in your communication. Authenticity is a salve that heals disconnection and makes you a magnet for healthy relationships. Notice when social conditioning overtakes your vulnerability. Is there a more honest part of yourself that is ready to be heard? Speak from your heart and you will open the gate for others to speak from theirs. Your trustworthiness will shine. Compassion and truth will be the defining qualities of your communications, serving as a much-needed balm to all of humanity.

Balanced: clear, authentic, direct, compassionate
Imbalanced: disharmony, mistrust, gossip
To bring into balance: communicate with honesty, vulnerability, and truth

Air

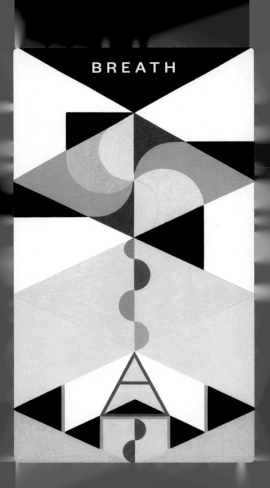

Breath

INSPIRATION   Breath is the vibratory note between the starting point of life and the still point of death. All activity derives from her flow. Your mother's breath is the first gift she gave you; it was passed down from her mother, and upon both of their respirations, you alighted upon the world. The strength of your connection with your own breath is the extent to which you are connected to your existence, creativity, and power. Breath is prayer and praise; she is all-inspiring.

Breath is a sign that inspiration is afoot. The words *breath* and *inspiration* are deeply entwined; they are integral to one another. To become inspired is to have an idea breathed into you as an exclamation from the divine. The inspiration you receive is a vision of reality that already exists, and it is yours to create if you so choose. Breathe into your inspiration and discover if it is right for you to embark upon it at this time.

Balanced: receptive to divinely sourced potentials

Imbalanced: lack of new ideas, enduring sameness

To bring into balance: practice purification through the control of your breath

BUTTERFLY

Butterfly

METAMORPHOSIS   The chrysalis trembles, a habitat palpitating with ardor. It is a theater of transformation materializing into form. With scales of painted wings, her pupal skin splits in two. This is an unwinding, enveloped by devout effort, through which an emergence takes place. Unencumbered by the limits of reason, her journey from caterpillar to Butterfly is complete. The next stage now awaits her. She is a queen, empowered by her ancestral credentials to perform wonders. She greets the world with new eyes, a lineage of greatness supporting her.

Butterfly's transformation was arduous. What courage it took to spin that cocoon knowing what was to come. She is here to remind you that your precious life force needn't be squandered on maintaining outdated versions of yourself; instead, use it for becoming an emanation of your spirit's purpose. Bewilderment during the metamorphosis process is normal. Breathe with this process. Meditate upon your present and future self as free, victorious, and soaring. Your time in the chrysalis asks you to draw upon your reserves of faith and courage, and these qualities will guide the way during your transformation.

Balanced: trust, self-care, surrender

Imbalanced: change-averse

To bring into balance: clear clutter, relinquish outdated beliefs

CLOUD

Cloud

RITUAL   Cloud arises when liquid droplets transform
into crystals suspended in time—he is a kindred of
many worlds. His vapor sings with celestial mobility,
networking our moods with higher thought. He clarifies
the scope of life's unpredictability with foils of wisps,
chains of ripples, and scrolls of futures. He is broad-
casting Earth's emotional intelligence to the cosmos
and precipitating galactic wisdom upon the planet. He
is a two-way mirror with the power to influence worlds.

Cloud invites you to create magic through ritual.
You can quickly usher in the change you desire by
designing daily or monthly ceremonies that invoke the
visions you hold for life. Cloud reminds you that the
world of the spirit and the physical realm are reflections
of one another. By crafting meaningful ritual, you join
both together to bring your vision alive. Your intentions
gather like water droplets, and you are empowered to
shower life-giving rain upon beautiful new realities.

Balanced: conscious creation

Imbalanced: perceptions of fixed realities that limit potential

To bring into balance: perform a simple ritual, invoking the full
participation of your sovereign, essential self

CRANE

Crane

LONGEVITY   Golden hues cut through the black night, imbuing the wetlands with suggestions of paradise. The morning light breaks over this austere terrain. It is home to the prestigious mystic, prince of all birds, Crane. He is a faithful mate and fills the reedy hollowness of the world with his devotion. He is streamlined and substantial, electrified in his longevity. Crane's stamina soars on his extravagant, outstretched wings. His lengthy migrations, thunderous calls, and grand physical stature are indications of a life lived with phosphorescent gusto.

Crane invites you to go the distance, and for this, he offers his blessings of longevity. By making the decision to see something all the way through, you are choosing to fill hollow areas with your love and devotion. You are choosing completeness. Life responds to your commitment in kind by increasing your energy reserves, strengthening your nervous system, opening your heart center, and aligning you with the relationships and resources you require to fulfill your soul's sacred mission.

Balanced: follow-through, ability to commit

Imbalanced: disinterested, unreliable, many incompletions

To bring into balance: choose a small project and finish it

EAGLE

Eagle

PERSPECTIVE   Eagle's domain is in the heights. He transcends the laws of velocity with his certainty, a performance unorthodox to the five senses. With the sky's blessing, this prideful raptor's glide allows him to see it all. From mountaintops to woodlands, he takes in his sovereign and privileged view, informed by instinct and guided by inner substance. He is restricted by nothing. His flight is extravagant because he claims his divinity with the sobriety of a saint; he is unfettered by pettiness or preference. He mates, nests, and hunts with the confidence of a clairvoyant, trusting that he has found his place in the universe.

Eagle asks you to hold the high watch. The sublime comes to you disguised as your life; this is the vantage point of the Eagle. For him, duality-based preferences have no relevance, and there is only source energy in full expression. Any initiation, boon, or boredom is a gift to your soul's evolution and growth. In this way, each trial and victory are the same thing. There is nothing in the world that can delay you from fulfilling your soul's primary purpose when you hold his aerial perspective.

Balanced: the ability to love all of one's life without the interference of preference

Imbalanced: aversive, pettiness

To bring into balance: spend an entire day suspending all opinions

FLYING FISH

Flying Fish

LEAP OF FAITH   Flying Fish gathers her liquid turquoise momentum before taking a leap of faith. She is soft-bodied sweetness, an outstretched plain of streamlined scales and winged fins—she is an improbability. Her transcendental gift to life is the disruption of inertia. Her forked tail beats rapidly, taxiing her across the sea's surface and building her courage before she ascends. Her reward is eternal self-confidence: she will repeat this marvel again and again. With each jump, she spans a great distance.

Flying Fish says it's time to make a leap of faith. Become an auteur of improbable victory. Claim the leading role in a fantastic dream. You can be a fish that flies. Everything is possible—even if it hasn't been achieved yet. Remember that Flying Fish does not go the entire distance with just one leap; her travels are the result of many successive jumps. Each choice is a launching pad for the next. Every leap of faith aligns you more with your vision.

Balanced: adventurousness, willingness to overcome fear, confidence

Imbalanced: lack of self-confidence

To bring into balance: step outside of your comfort zone

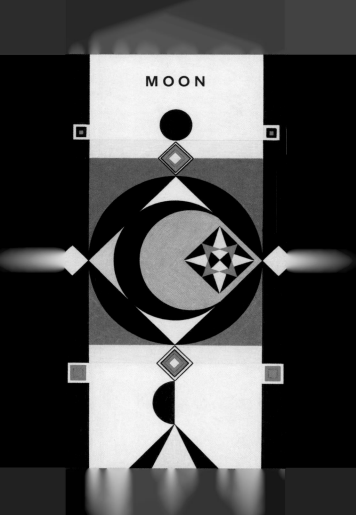

MOON

Moon

DEVOTION   Moon orbits the Earth with devotional influence. Her phases symbolize immortality and eternality. She pulls and pushes with benevolent force, maintaining steadfast, universal alignment for all. Moon shapes tides and stone, blood and bone, while the luminosity she offers stabilizes planetary climates and imbues us with the wisdom of her ebb and flow. Like the goddess herself, she is ardent and tender, a perfect reflection of light and a natural amplifier of dark.

Moon summons your devotion. Your orbit is profound and necessary, your intrinsic merit nourishes the lives of many, even if you don't realize it. Moon asks you to take stock of where you are placing your loyalty. Is your devotional energy aligned with your values and desires? If so, Moon invites you to deepen into your commitment with the conviction that the returns will be great. If not, Moon asks you to reorient your gravitational pull to align with more fruitful uses of your devotion.

Balanced: nourished by your efforts, skillful loyalty
Imbalanced: putting precious energy into a void, loyalty without reciprocity
To bring into balance: notice where you feel depleted in life and shift priorities

Moth

CLAIRVOYANCE   Light enters each beat of her wings, pushing Moth into a realm of luminosity. She is a paradox, one who negotiates inky obscuration yet lives for the light. This valued keeper of elemental balance is the mother of unconditional ethos, untangling programs of the past into sweet resolve and purity of purpose. She entices the soul to reveal the deeper meaning of her own existence, the sum total of all lifetimes lived before. Awash in elucidation, she understands that this embodiment is the most profound of them all; it is the living library of each of her previous incarnations.

Moth whispers for you to trust your knowing even if others wish to persuade you of different realities. Like Moth, our clairvoyance flies through the night of ignorance and forgetting, headed wholeheartedly toward illumination, toward the light of truth. You will know whether you are experiencing authentic clairvoyance when you become still and allow the information to permeate your entirety, finding that it is validated by the coherent agreement of your body, heart and mind. While the truth may cause you to stretch—which can sometimes be uncomfortable—it always feels like a move toward authentic liberation.

Balanced: reliable, intuition-based access to truth
Imbalanced: pulled in different directions by conflicting voices
To bring into balance: gravitate toward the thoughts that offer liberation from suffering

OWL

Owl

MESSENGER   Owl is solitary, nocturnal, upright, and sharp. He is eccentric; of his four toes, three point forward to where he is going and one points back to where he has been. He sees through darkness. His head also offers a wide range of mobility so he can see his full environment with ease. The low frequency of his vocalizations cuts through the velvet of night, and he swoops on soft wings, stealthy and cryptic. A symbol of paranormal wisdom, Owl offers messages for you to dissect and interpret on a subconscious level so they can serve your conscious choices.

Owl is a messenger. With his penchant for prophecy, he announces change and is a strong spirit guide when you need help understanding the obscure elements in your life. He helps you release the tangible and move into the imaginative. What truth are you avoiding? What clarity has been muddled by wishful thinking? What words have you been unable to say for fear of alienation from all that is structured and known? What lives in the darkness that you've pretended doesn't exist? Call upon Owl's medicine to cut through the night. Trust his message; it will lead you toward the light.

Balanced: clear knowing

Imbalanced: confusion, obscuration

To bring into balance: seek out solitude and go within to hear your inner calling through meditative introspection

RAY OF LIGHT

Ray of Light

FOCUS   Ray of Light offers speedy luminosity. His bright spectrum beams wide, a fundamental constant of nature that allows us to see and understand our world. His reasoning polarizes everything in his path, intensifying exactness and focusing on the impalpable. Out of him, we create realities. In his brightness, all inhibitions subside, all uncertainties fall away. What was once blurred focuses with sharp clarity, aligning your perspectives with omniscience.

Ray of Light reminds you that where your attention goes, energy flows. Your consciousness is a light ray, imbuing life-giving nourishment to everything it highlights. What you emphasize with your awareness can either enhance or deplete your quality of life. Ask Ray of Light to help you focus on your vision for the future rather than your fears. See your dreams coming into form. Imagine the tastes, smells, and colors coalescing into a world where you want to live. Ray of Light loves to amplify convictions of beauty.

Balanced: able to visualize positive outcomes and bring them into form

Imbalanced: fixated upon what one doesn't want

To bring into balance: fiercely redirect your attention

Fire

Bee

DEFIANCE   She is the hymn of the flower family, a social insect of intricate memory and impeccable taste. Physically speaking, she should not be able to fly, yet she defies the laws of aerodynamics. Winged magnate of nectar and holy diviner of ambrosia, Bee bathes in pollen and spreads her message far and wide. Bee moves beyond her limitations, her life an object lesson in overcoming the impossible.

Often our life's momentum originates from the harsh push of our fears rather than the magnetic pull of our dreams. When this happens, we succumb to our collective histories of limitation. Bee says that this is your time to express healthy defiance. Streamline your behavior to reflect where you're going, not where you've been. Sip sweetness from the flowers that speak directly to your heart rather than the ones you are drawn to by habit, and, like Bee, you will be magically upheld on a trajectory to success.

Balanced: sustained focus, joyful effort, bold breakthroughs

Imbalanced: fear of failure, barren of hope

To bring into balance: hold a boundary that protects the momentum toward your vision

DESERT

Desert

ADAPT   Desert can be unforgiving, but his extreme
conditions shatter heavy concepts that might try to
limit our light. His starkness and absence of shadows
scrub us of prescribed beliefs and elicit the drive to
go inward for answers. Scintillating night skies offer
a foil for the austerity of his endless expanse. He is a
threatening terrain, calling forth the self-sufficiency and
adaptability of the resident flora and fauna. Vast and
unpopulated, Desert is also a magnet for seekers of
clarity, revelation, and purity.

Desert's extreme climate forces you to adapt.
There is often a gap between the recognition about
a need for change and the perfect timing to initiate it.
Change will come. Meanwhile, make yourself comfort-
able by working amicably with your circumstances.
The benefits of doing so will extend beyond this
window of time. Just as certain Desert animals survive
by burrowing into the earth or growing thick skins, your
adaptation skills will open the door to lifelong satisfaction, no matter what's going on around you.

Balanced: adaptable, a sense of unshakable well-being

Imbalanced: fidgeting in one's own skin, palpable discomfort
until ideal circumstances are achieved

To bring into balance: surrender to your circumstances,
the support will arise

LADYBUG

Ladybug

MIRACLE   When European farmers prayed to Mother Mary for a miracle to protect their vulnerable crops, Ladybug arrived to devour the pests. The farmers, surprised that divine intervention could come in such an unsuspecting form, called her "Beetle of Our Lady," and we know her now as Ladybug.

Ladybug signifies a miracle. But remember, when you expect help to appear in a specific form, her gift can sometimes be overlooked, so keep an open mind. Divine assistance is improvisational, playful, and surprising; it is a lucid discovery, like tiny Ladybugs saving a whole season of crops. The same goes for the miracles that await you. Prepare for the possibility that they will be just as unexpected as they are mighty.

Balanced: receptive to unexpected forms of support

Imbalanced: holding rigid expectations that block magical interventions

To bring into balance: practice playfulness as a magnet for divine intervention

LAVA

Lava

COURAGE Volcanoes are portals to the heart of our Earth, ablaze with emotional fire. When they erupt, Lava pours forth, covering the old and outdated while forging new pathways. Lava scorches everything in her path, a searing field of anger. But when she cools, she forms dynamic new landscapes that are fertilized by nutrient-rich ash.

Lava guides you to locate the fiery core within yourself. This period of change and transformation requires courage. It is important to access your internal magma and the deep desire that brought you where you are. You must hold yourself steady while old and un-useful paths and ideas are consumed around you. Once your molten courage cools, the past is simply a prologue and the future transforms into a lush and fertile landscape, waiting for something new to take root and thrive.

Balanced: determined, courageous

Imbalanced: averse to experiencing the intensity of life

To bring into balance: have a ceremony and ask nature for inspiration, guidance, and guardianship

LION

Lion

JUSTICE   Lion is the native ruler of his tribal kingship, the apex predator of his territory. His prominent mane demands authority. His pride is ruled by balance. His message of prudence bellows for all to hear, a clear oracle of justice. He can be heard from miles away and the force of his sound immortalizes his presence as emperor. Like all great leaders, Lion strives for peace and order within his dominion with quick and decisive ferocity and his own innate grace.

Lion is present when justice is required. Hardwired within our DNA is the felt experience of fairness and equity—it is written in our bones. We sense when it's present and when it's missing. This knowing can be obstructed by the interferences of the world, and we might talk ourselves out of speaking truth because of the false perception that our voice doesn't make a difference. Lion invites you to tap into the prevailing potency of his roar when advocating for justice.

Balanced: prevailing justice, willingness to speak up

Imbalanced: fear of disrupting the order of the "old guard"

To bring into balance: tune in to your essential self and envision a deep intellectual cleansing of all strong opinions living in your awareness

PHOENIX

Phoenix

RESURRECTION   He is a pillar of eternal light, presenting vital passages of cyclical regeneration. Phoenix is always transforming through birth, death, and resurrection. When everything that once was is no longer, he activates rebirth through fire and fortitude. Once he has offered his complete existence to the sacred flames, a new Phoenix emerges out of the ash, and he arises, young and powerful. The new Phoenix is an emanation of his ancestors' labor and wisdom— refreshed and ready to give his gifts to the world.

Phoenix sends the message that a part of your life is undergoing resurrection. He facilitates the inward journey that is necessary before any rebirth—nothing real can ever be lost. Let his medicine lay claim to all that is no longer relevant to your ever-evolving exis- tence. Surrender yourself to the fire of renewal and you will return reborn, refined, and with more beauty and power than you could have possibly imagined.

Balanced: relaxed and trusting of the process

Imbalanced: inner conflict with what is

To bring into balance: allow yourself to grieve what has ended, deep rest

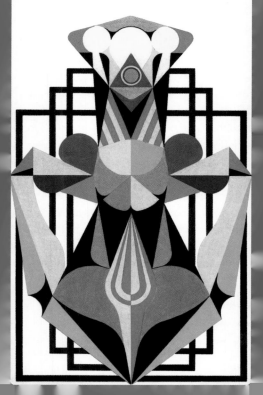

PRAYING MANTIS

Praying Mantis

MEDITATION   Difficult to spot as she rests in the leaves, Praying Mantis is revered for her ability to remain still. When she does move, she steps deliberately; nothing is done without intuitive verification, which assures her safety and success. In this way, Praying Mantis communes with otherworldly modalities of truth. In her world, the unforeseen does not exist; rooted in the stillness of her rumination, she remains open and certain, a prophet of tranquility.

Praying Mantis appears when the medicine of meditation is most required. The more complex life gets, the more you will benefit from the truth offered by your inner sage. The price for this wisdom is to immerse yourself in the calm waters that exist beneath the waves of worldly distractions. Make space for the voice within to speak. Praying Mantis will guide you toward stillness and clarity; this is her territory.

Balanced: informed by internal wisdom
Imbalanced: frenetically driven by the ebb and flow of the outer world

To bring into balance: stillness and meditation

SCORPION

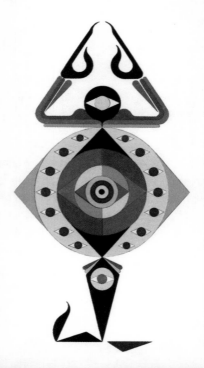

Scorpion

PASSION   Priestess of harsh climes and mysteries of the night, Scorpion is an astrological jewel and enchantress. Her biological brilliance is draped in self-reliance and dangerous protective forces. As a potent guardian of the mythical and unordinary, she expresses ardor for her life as an enthusiastic lover, protective mother, and skilled hunter. By keeping the balance between solitude and lustiness, the sting of desire becomes eternally irresistible; her passion transcends the sexual and enters the realm of holy creation.

Scorpion medicine arrives when you need to recommit to your passion for earthly life. The soul evolves through your bodily experiences, which are adorned by many wholesome pleasures. It's time to embrace them. With her deadly defenses, Scorpion is not encumbered by a fear of passion. In fact, it is her attraction to intensity that keeps her safe. Call upon Scorpion when your own passion feels pale and allow her to guide you through the night toward the dawning of fresh enthusiasm for your human experience.

Balanced: passion for life

Imbalanced: timid, lackluster, prevailing ennui

To bring into balance: rekindle the meditative flames of your ancestral relationships and ask the ones who came before you for instruction, protection, and supervision

SUN

Sun

DIVINE SERVICE   As the star at the center of our solar system, a fiery traveler of timeless confidence and force, Sun unifies the planets through gravity and light. Illuminating and supreme, he devours the shadows. His circulating heat is all-powerful and offers the understanding that to honor the divine within and all around us, we must all serve.

Sun reveals that by giving undivided attention to your inner luminosity, you free it to shine outward, illuminating the way for others. This is the way of life—we evolve to serve. Just as Sun's light serves all life on Earth, your light serves all whom you know. Continue to invigorate your inner light so that you become a pharos of clarity and wisdom. This is not a purely selfless path. As you offer your service, its radiating warmth is reflected back by all who benefit, and you are remunerated in multiples.

Balanced: serving from a place of wholeness

Imbalanced: selfishness, self-serving attitudes, self-sacrifice

To bring into balance: develop the art of gracefully receiving to instill the felt sense of what it's like to accept from others openly—and then give in return

THUNDERBOLT

Thunderbolt

DISPELLING IGNORANCE   Weapon of the sky, Thunderbolt is the conductor of consequence. Full-throated and unswerving, this electric iconoclast reigns with force, leveling resistance and dispelling ignorance. Though he seems destructive, his temper plays a part in the evolution of much of Earth's life-forms. He has equal power to annihilate and bestow life; the moment he hits is an instant of synthesis, disrupting tightly held notions and lighting the way for new truths to emerge.

Thunderbolt does not hold back his fervent proclamations, telling you that the difficulty is not in the issue itself but rather in how you currently choose to see things. Ignorance is at the root of all suffering and arises from misperception about the nature of existence. This noxious obstacle to freedom can be overcome with little effort once you cease clinging to limiting and damaging ideas. Call upon Thunderbolt to grace your perceptions with his sonic shock wave. Ask him to transform your perspective into a freshly seen, world-churned, mind-blown experience that elevates all of your relationships.

Balanced: illumined, open-minded, content

Imbalanced: suffering through misperception, craving or aversive

To bring into balance: question the indoctrinations that cause your suffering

Ether

PEGASUS

Pegasus

FREEDOM   Born of the sea, Pegasus is a goddess mare with triumphant angel wings; she is a master at uniting the cosmic and earthly realms. Dressed as a warrior luminary, this noble equine rules the open skies and visits as you slumber. She is a defender of liberty, willing to carry you above the clouds of the familiar toward your soaring dreams of freedom. She imbues all she encounters with her healing frequencies and offers loyal companionship to those who respect innocence.

Pegasus willingly presents what is possible for the evolution of your soul. She is here to escort you into a vast new sense of freedom. Now is the time to declare to the universe that you are complete with your limitations. If you are tangled in a thought or emotion that is holding you back, this is the moment to release it. If you are in a circumstance that you have clearly outgrown, here is the sign that you're ready to move forward. If you are indulging in a habit that you know drains your energy, now is the moment to put it aside. Call upon Pegasus and allow her to take you to the heights of her choosing. All you must do is accept her reins.

Balanced: connection to one's infinite potential

Imbalanced: lack, limitation, addiction, feeling trapped

To bring into balance: adopt a willingness to release self-limiting beliefs and habits

RAINBOW

Rainbow

ABUNDANCE AND NEW OPPORTUNITY   Rainbow is a promise kept brought to life in the glorious after-math of the storm. He is the spellbinding reflection of unseen particles dancing in the ethers, positioned for all of us to witness and absorb. Wrapping you in his complexion of seven mystical colors, Rainbow's serene vibrancy illuminates inclusiveness and cohesion, unwrapping a very important message of fortune.

Rainbow rewards you with a vast reminder of your own glowing horizon. He is a powerful indicator that suffering and scarcity are never the final destination and that your birthright is a continuously replenished wellspring of abundance and new opportunity. Now is the time to cross the bridge and unlock the false perceptions of your hindrances so you may surrender them to the light and receive the blessings that are ready to reveal themselves to you.

Balanced: renewed optimism after a trial

Imbalanced: stuck in the despair of the aftermath of destruction

To bring into balance: find your creative flow within each moment so that you become connected to your authentic expression without altering yourself to please others

SAGE

Sage

PURIFICATION   She willingly transforms into ember in the name of sacramental cleansing. She is a living ceremony, charged with protection and the unmitigated desire to let go. She burns, clarifying and cleansing interference and toxic spirits from her surroundings. She purifies all—even herself. Sage is native to high-desert ecosystems and perfectly embodies their grounding qualities. With your aligned intentions, she will gladly hasten your positive transitions and clarify your purpose and vision.

Sage indicates the timeliness of purification. With your intention to clear cluttered energies from the spaces of your body, mind, emotions, home, and altar, she will, by her ashen, solemn plume, unveil a new blessing. Enlist Sage to accelerate your purification process. Ask her to surge toward your senses with her delicate strains of perfumed smoke. The overall clarity and groundedness that this ritual brings will be its own reward.

Balanced: clear, harmonious, grounded

Imbalanced: depressed, chaotic, conflicting energies that create confusion

To bring into balance: intentionally clear your physical spaces every day

SCARAB

Scarab

SECOND CHANCE   Born of noble bloodlines, Scarab is a bold and dreamlike harbinger of rebirth. The Egyptian god Khepri wears a Scarab crown each morning as he calls forth the sun, eliciting a sigh of gratitude across the planet for the new day. In this daily work of rebirthing the solar deity again and again, Scarab reflects your own infinite supply of second chances. Enveloping you with the possibilities of past, present, and future, the cycle of death and rebirth is his gift to our evolution.

As a premier companion for second chances, Scarab appears when the material world dissolves. He is here to hold your hand and help you take flight into the uncharted. Life is unstoppable and every ending comes with a built-in beginning. All sunsets lead to sunrise. Everything ends, but in some form, there will always be an opportunity to do it again with greater refinement, satisfaction, and excellence. Face your judgment willingly and with greater faculties: your victory over death is eternal.

Balanced: faith in your ability to heal and willingness to see life's inherent talent for self-renewal

Imbalanced: flattened by a perception of terminal defeat

To bring into balance: align with nature's rhythms of advancement and retreat, honor your primal instincts

Sky

LUCIDITY   Expansive and inviting, Sky holds all of the universe's magnificence, meanings, and history. He offers safe passage for the truth of light and invites unmitigated participation in universal evolution. Sky's thoughts are vaporous clouds that move along unburdened by concepts; he neither rejects nor clings to anything. He is simple, clear, eternal awareness. We can look up and ask him anything. He listens without judgment and answers all questions.

Sky offers advice to practice discernment when it comes to believing your own thoughts and the thoughts of others. Thoughts are mercurial, mutable, and transient. We empower them to become reality when we join them with our emotions—the union of thought and feeling is how we shape our worlds. To make room for fresh potential and luminous inspiration, it is important to declutter your mind on a regular basis. Doing so will provide you with great lucidity and open the door to your own, sky-like expansiveness. Welcome the boundless opportunities.

Balanced: spacious, voluminous, intuitive, open-minded

Imbalanced: constricted by limiting thoughts, fearful, fixated

To bring into balance: sky-gaze by resting on the earth and neutrally watching the clouds roll by as if they were thoughts; differentiate between the inherently vast nature of the mind and the conditioned thoughts that often obscure it

SNAKE

Snake

THE HEALING SPIRAL   Snake is the fertile union between ebb and flow. She willingly lives life's experiences, then releases them back to the earth when they no longer serve her existence, shedding her skin regularly to release and be born anew. When resting, Snake forms a coiled spiral, soaking in the warmth from the earth, bringing herself into balance and healing.

Sometimes it might feel like you are just going in circles, revisiting old patterns or wounds you thought were healed, but Snake indicates that this can be positive. Her body forms circles within circles, a reminder that healing happens in a spiral and what we thought we left behind must sometimes be revisited for healing to be complete. While Snake's spiraling energy might journey toward the stars, her actual body rests against the Earth. Snake reminds you to spend time resting your own body on the ground. Close your eyes and receive the Earth's frequencies. Stay focused on your vision of wholeness. You are making progress, even if it sometimes appears you are just going in circles.

Balanced: patience, forbearance of concrete conclusions, easy flow

Imbalanced: frozen, hopeless, a perception of fixed dis-ease

To bring into balance: retune yourself to Earth's biorhythms and allow them to assist your return to wholeness by spending time resting your body on the soft ground

SPIDER

Spider

TRUST   Spider weaves her silken, life-supporting matrix with precision and purpose. The story is that Spider's web intercepts her prey, but this is misperception. She is an inspired creatrix, her web intentionally birthed to attract rather than trap. Her success comes from trusting that the magnetism of her artistry will carry her through.

Spider teaches a primal truth about the willingness to trust that the tools you have within will awaken your untapped capabilities. It is not only safe to live from your inspiration; it is advisable. When you weave your world out of passion rather than obligation, your authentic creativity and purpose are unleashed. You become a lightning rod for grace. Take a page from Spider's book and trust your passion and artistry as a portal for your prosperity.

Balanced: inspired, creative, innovative

Imbalanced: dogmatic adherence to the expectations of others

To bring into balance: commit to your creative process

STAR

Star

DIVINE GUIDANCE   He adorns the indigo night like phosphorescent pearls, transforming a directionless abyss with his radiating pinpoints of supernatural guidance. Star's embroidered constellations are the embodiment of self-reliance, helping you navigate toward your own bright future.

Star appears when the path is obscured and you need a nudge in the right direction. When you ask for guidance, the universe will certainly answer. Listen and look for the clues that are offered; there is always a way through. Spend time under the stars at night and let them remind you that you are a beloved member of the cosmos, one who shines among many.

Balanced: able to discern true guidance

Imbalanced: pulled in myriad directions

To bring into balance: reconnect with the sun's cycle; wake at dawn and keep your day flowing organically, without hesitation

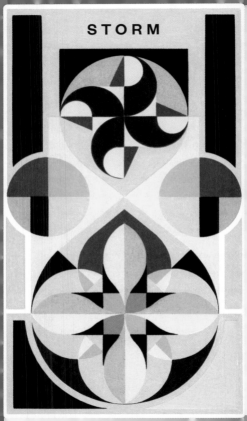

Storm

TRANSITION   She is the cycle of madness necessary to reclaim serenity. Before Storm's arrival, the gathering charge expands, creating deep unrest. She weaves her rumble of thunder with flashes of lightning, commanding immediate attention. Her climactic performance echoes through the theater of the gods, opening new dimensions. Finally, the skies rain down the tears that precede tomorrow's renewal.

Storm indicates transition. In the midst of the tempest, you might wonder how much damage will be done or even whether you will survive. Remember that the polarity of destruction is renewal—one does not exist without the other. How you endure the storm will influence your ability to regenerate once it's over. Now is the time to take exquisite care of yourself. Soon the sun will be out, the air will be fresh and full of vitality, and a new world will be revealed.

Balanced: confidence in one's resiliency

Imbalanced: trepidation in the midst of change

To bring into balance: stabilize your body's electrical environment by embracing the theory of grounding

WIND

Wind

BREATHWORK Weightless and invisible, Wind holds the secrets of all that came before this moment and all that will arise. She is air in its most active form—creating patterns by drawing in and releasing. She brings fresh energy to multidimensional pursuits and helps clear up insoluble problems. Her significance in the body is to serve as an ambassador between physical and spirit realms, sustaining life force in the form of breath.

Wind is a reminder of the transformative power of breathwork. Whether you resonate with morning breathing meditations or simply commit to bringing more awareness into your breath throughout the day, there is no faster way to transform both your immediate and long-term realities. Just as a strong breeze clears the air, breathing with intention helps process emotions, release stuck energy, cleanse blood, reinforce the soul's stabilization within the body, and tune in to a more conscious way of perceiving the world. Though there are both elaborate and simple ways to harness the power of your breath, your intention to connect with this powerful force is what brings about transformation.

Balanced: habitually enlisting breath to move easefully

Imbalanced: unconsciously holding the breath, blocked emotions and numbness

To bring into balance: bring regular, simple awareness to your breath

Wild
Cards

Divine Feminine

FULFILLMENT   As the breath of the untouched and the bearer of wildernesses, she is the Divine Feminine, eternally in service to everlasting beauty. The sacred polarity between the Divine Feminine and Divine Masculine is responsible for the totality of existence and lives within each of us, regardless of how we identify ourselves within our own body. Her role is the unfolding discovery of the heart merged with the purity of her counterpart's ever-evolving wonderment. Divine Feminine is ceremonial in bliss, a consecrated womb of no-thing from which all things are born. She is the mystery, the void, the abyss, the ecstatic fulfillment of worlds, and the absolute essence of the universe.

Divine Feminine announces that something is ready to be fulfilled. Divine Feminine is the voice that assures you will have everything you need to develop and birth your vision, dreams, and desires. There is no better time than now to declare your resounding "yes" to the creative endeavor that is calling your name.

Balanced: openness to fulfilling divine inspiration and ideas

Imbalanced: stuck in false perceptions of inadequacy or lack

To bring into balance: begin the creation process, even if you feel frightened

DIVINE

MASCULINE

Divine Masculine

PRESENCE   Resonant with electricity and extraordinary skill, Divine Masculine enlists his perfect mind to gallantly deliver creative instruction. He harmonizes his influence with Divine Feminine's untouched omnipresence, giving rise to the exquisite individuality that characterizes all life. This sacred polarity between the Divine Masculine and Divine Feminine is responsible for the totality of existence and lives within each of us, regardless of how we identify ourselves within our own body.

Divine Masculine indicates that your full presence is required. By simply aligning your unfractured consciousness with the moment, you supply healing, balancing truths and conjure new possibilities and outcomes. It is much easier to receive a message from your inner Divine Masculine wisdom when you anchor your full presence within each moment. Practice this, and you will soon discover a secret: you are a painter of galaxies and legend of the real.

Balanced: harmonious attunement with self, others, and surroundings

Imbalanced: cognitive dissonance, lack of connection to the greater world

To bring into balance: remove distractions and become fully present in the moment; do only one thing at a time

About
the Deck

About the Art

Nature and her elements are inextricable from the divination of creativity.

Drawn from the depths of the inner workings of all the elements, I meditated on their intelligence and purpose while creating the art and words for these cards. I was guided by Mother Earth on a journey into the nature of life in its simplest, yet most complex forms. And, within her menagerie of wonders, I discovered my own connection with her truths. These drawings came out of that intimate bond.

Through this offering, we all have an opportunity to align with the higher power that is inherent within each of us. We are guided by the elements to travel back to the primordial still point, to our own heart space, which is always resonating with the devotional sincerity of universal love. I hope you find as much meaning and guidance when working with this deck as I did in creating it.